THE NEW
KIDS'
COOKBOOK

KÖNEMANN

The New Kids' Cookbook

Set of mixing bowls

Measuring jug

Chopping board

Dish towel

Strainer

Baking dish

Measuring cups

Scissors

Grater

Spatula

Sharp knife

Fork

Potato peeler

Ice-cream scoop

Pastry brush

Small saucepan

Wooden spoon

Measuring spoons

Oven mitts

2

Before you start...

Cooking is lots of fun, but you need to get organized. Before you try any of the recipes in this book, there are a few things to know.

❁ Always ask an adult for permission before you start cooking.

❁ Wash your hands well with soap and water, and wear an apron to protect your clothes.

❁ Always wear oven mitts to remove anything from the oven or microwave.

❁ Be careful with pots and pans on the stove. Turn the handles in, so you don't knock them off, and hold the handle when you are stirring anything, so the pan doesn't slip.

❁ Put hot pans and dishes on a chopping board when you take them off the heat or out of the oven.

❁ Don't test hot food with your fingers—press gently with the back of a spoon to test for doneness. If you do burn yourself, hold your hand under cold water.

❁ Remember to turn off the oven, the burner or gas when you have finished using it.

❁ If you are not used to handling sharp knives, ask an adult to help you chop things. Always use a chopping board—not the bench or table, and never hold a knife by the blade.

❁ Read the recipe right through before you start , and make sure you have everything you need. Set out all the ingredients and utensils on the kitchen table or bench.

❁ Recipes in this book are graded to help you learn; if you are just starting, try the easy ones (with one chef's hat), then move up.

Snacks & drinks

Speedy Sausage Rolls

Preparation time: 20 minutes
Cooking time: 15 minutes **Makes:** 16

INGREDIENTS
16 cocktail sausages
2 sheets puff pastry
milk, for glazing
tomato ketchup, for dipping

UTENSILS
sharp knife
pastry brush
baking sheets
oven mitts

Put out everything you need for this recipe on the countertop or table. Turn oven on to moderately hot 415°F.

1 Separate sausages, if necessary.

2 Cut each sheet of pastry into four strips. Cut each strip crossways in half to give 16 rectangles altogether.

3 Put a sausage on the end of one rectangle of pastry.

Roll up to enclose sausage. Brush end of pastry with milk, press down on join to seal. Put roll, join-side down, on baking sheet. Repeat with rest of sausages and pastry.

4 Using the point of a sharp knife, make four shallow slits across top of each roll. Brush rolls with milk. Bake for 15 minutes or until golden brown. Serve with a bowl of tomato ketchup.

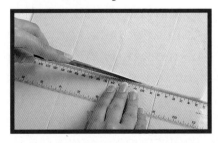

Cut each sheet of pastry into four strips, then cut each strip in half crossways.

Gingerbread Cookies

Preparation time: 50 minutes
Cooking time: 15 minutes **Makes:** about 24

INGREDIENTS
melted butter or oil
1/4 cup dark corn syrup
5 tablespoons butter
1/2 cup light brown sugar
1 egg
2 cups all-purpose flour
1/4 cup self-rising flour
1 teaspoon baking soda
3 teaspoons ground ginger
2 teaspoons currants

Icing
1 1/4 cups confectioners' sugar
2 teaspoons butter, melted
1–2 tablespoons water
different food colorings
candies, to decorate

UTENSILS
baking sheets
jug
small pan
measuring cups and spoons
3 mixing bowls
electric mixer
kitchen paper
rolling pin
gingerbread cutter
spatula
strainer or fine sieve
oven mitts
wooden spoon

 Put out everything you need for this recipe on the countertop or table.
Turn oven on to moderate 350°F. Grease baking sheets with melted butter or oil.

1 Put syrup in jug and stand jug in pan of hot tapwater until syrup is warm and soft.

2 Put butter and sugar in one of the mixing bowls and mix with mixer or spoon until creamy.

3 Separate the egg. Stir yolk into bowl with butter and sugar mixture.

4 In another mixing bowl, sift flours, soda and ginger. Slowly add flour mixture and syrup to butter and sugar, mixing well.

5 Take mixture out of bowl and place on counter. Knead lightly. Roll out with a rolling pin to 2 inches thick.

The New Kids' Cookbook

6 Using gingerbread or animal shaped cutters, cut out cookies. Carefully lift them onto greased baking sheets with a spatula. Place currants into cookies for eyes.

7 Put baking sheets in oven and cook for 15 minutes. Turn off oven, take out sheets and cool for 15 minutes.

8 To make Icing: Mix confectioners' sugar, butter and water in small bowl. Divide mixture into several small bowls. Color each icing mixture differently. Pipe or drizzle icings to decorate cookies. Use icing to glue lollies for decoration. Ice one cookie at a time, as the icing sets quickly.

Crispy Herb and Garlic Bread

Preparation time: 10 minutes
Cooking time: 3 minutes **Serves:** 4

INGREDIENTS
2 oblong rolls
2 tablespoons butter,
  softened
1 clove garlic, crushed
1 tablespoon chopped fresh
  basil

UTENSILS
sharp knife
measuring spoons
small bowl
knife

 Put out everything you need for this recipe on the countertop or table.
Turn broiler on to high.
1 Cut rolls in half lengthways.
2 Mix butter, garlic and basil in the bowl.
3 Broil uncut side of rolls for 1 minute or until brown.
4 Spread cut side with butter mixture, broil for 1 minute or until brown.

Notes: The bread should be cooked just before serving, but garlic butter can be made ahead and frozen for up to three months. Thaw before spreading it on the bread.
❂ To make a more special snack, broil the uncut side of the rolls, as above, spread the cut side with the butter mixture and top each with a slice of Cheddar cheese and half a slice of chopped bacon. Broil for 2 minutes or until bacon is crisp and brown.

Peanut Chocolate Chip Cookies

Preparation time: 20 minutes
Cooking time: 20 minutes **Makes:** about 20

INGREDIENTS
melted butter or oil, for
  greasing
1 cup self-rising flour
1 cup chocolate chips
1/2 cup chopped, roasted,
  unsalted peanuts
1/2 cup sugar
2 tablespoons butter
1/4 cup peanut butter
1 egg, lightly beaten
extra chocolate chips for top

UTENSILS
pastry brush
two 13 x 11 inch cookie sheets
waxed paper
sifter
large mixing bowl
measuring spoons
wooden spoon
small saucepan
oven mitts

 Put out everything you need for this recipe on the countertop or table. Turn oven on to moderate 350°F.

Brush cookie sheets with melted butter or oil and line bases with waxed paper.

1 Sift flour into mixing bowl. Put in chocolate chips, peanuts and sugar, stir well. Make a hole in the center.

2 Put butter and peanut butter in a small pan. Stir over low heat until butter has melted; remove from heat, cool slightly.

3 Pour butter mixture and egg into dry ingredients. Stir until just combined.

4 Drop level tablespoons of mixture onto cookie sheets, leaving room to spread. Bake for 20 minutes or until cookies are golden brown. Let them cool on sheets.

5 Melt extra chocolate chips in a bowl over hot water and put one spoonful on top of each cookie.

11

Strawberry Banana Shake

Preparation time: 5 minutes
Cooking time: nil **Serves:** 2

INGREDIENTS
1 small, ripe banana, chopped
1/2 cup chopped strawberries
1 cup milk
3 scoops ice-cream

UTENSILS
measuring cups
sharp knife
ice-cream scoop
blender or food processor

1 Put banana, strawberries, milk and ice-cream in blender or food processor bowl.
2 Blend on high speed for 1 minute or until mixture is smooth; pour into serving glasses.

Raspberry Yogurt Smoothie

Preparation time: 5 minutes
Cooking time: nil **Serves:** 3

INGREDIENTS
1 cup milk
1/2 cup raspberry yogurt
1 cup frozen raspberries

UTENSILS
measuring cups
blender or food processor

1 Combine milk, yogurt and raspberries in a blender or food processor.
2 Blend on high for 1 minute or until smooth. Pour into serving glasses.

Note: Frozen raspberries make the smoothie thick and cold.

Strawberry Banana Shake (right) and Raspberry Yogurt Smoothie.

Chocolate Malted Milk Shake

Preparation time: 5 minutes
Cooking time: nil **Serves:** 2

INGREDIENTS
1 cup milk
1 tablespoon instant
  chocolate drink mix
1 tablespoon powdered malt
  or 4 tablespoons chocolate
4 scoops ice-cream

UTENSILS
measuring cup
blender or food processor
ice-cream scoop

1 Put milk, chocolate, malt and ice-cream in blender or food processor bowl.
2 Blend mixture on high 1 minute or until all ingredients are combined. Pour into glasses and serve.

Mango Wizz

Preparation time: 5 minutes
Cooking time: nil **Serves:** 1

INGREDIENTS
1¹/₂ cups chopped fresh
  mango
¹/₂ cup ice cubes

UTENSILS
blender or food processor
measuring cup

**Chocolate Malted Milk Shake
(left) and Mango Wizz.**

1 Place ice cubes in blender or food processor bowl. Process until ice is roughly chopped.
2 Add mango. Process until fruit and ice are well combined. Pour mixture into a tall glass and serve straight away.

15

Griddle Cakes with Jam and Cream

Preparation time: 15 minutes
Cooking time: 10 minutes **Makes:** about 12

INGREDIENTS
3/4 cup self-rising flour
2 tablespoons sugar
1 egg, lightly beaten
1/2 cup milk
1 teaspoon butter, melted
jam, whipped cream, to
  serve

UTENSILS
sifter
medium mixing bowl
measuring spoons
wooden spoon
whisk
pastry brush
large frying pan
spatula

 Put out everything you need for this recipe on the countertop or table.

1 Sift flour into the bowl and stir in sugar. Make a hole in the center.

2 Mix egg and milk and add to flour all at once. Whisk until all the liquid is mixed in and the batter is smooth.

3 Brush bottom of the pan lightly with melted butter. Drop heaped tablespoons of mixture onto base of pan about 3/4 inch apart.

4 Cook over medium heat for 1 minute or until the underside is golden and the top is bubbly. Turn griddle cakes over, using a spatula. Cook 1 minute more or until golden on the other side.

5 Take griddle cakes out of pan; repeat with remaining mixture, allow griddle cakes to cool. Serve with jam and whipped cream.

Note: Griddle cakes taste best when fresh. Spread them with your favorite jam.

Muffin Pizzas

Preparation time: 20 minutes
Cooking time: 15 minutes **Serves:** 4

INGREDIENTS
4 English muffins
1/4 cup tomato paste

Salami and Cheese Topping
4 slices salami, chopped
1 green onion, chopped
1/3 cup grated mature
  Cheddar
1/2 teaspoon dried mixed
  herbs

**Bacon and Pineapple
  Topping**
1 slice bacon, chopped
half 7 oz can crushed
  pineapple, drained
1/3 cup grated mozzarella
  or mature Cheddar
1 tablespoon grated
  Parmesan cheese

UTENSILS
sharp knife
can opener
grater
colander
oven mitts

 Put out everything you need for this recipe on the countertop or table.
Turn oven on to moderately hot 415°F.
1 Split muffins in half. Spread cut side with tomato paste.
2 Top muffins with ingredients from either of the topping variations.
3 Put muffins on a baking sheet. Bake for 15 minutes or until golden brown.

Notes: Muffin Pizzas are best eaten while they are still hot.
❂ Add any of your other favorite pizza toppings, such as sliced mushrooms, chopped bell pepper, sliced tomato or chopped ham, if you like.

Butterscotch Melts

Preparation time: 20 minutes
Cooking time: 15 minutes **Makes:** about 18

INGREDIENTS
melted butter or oil
4 tablespoons butter
2 tablespoons light brown
  sugar
3/4 cup self-rising flour
1/4 cup custard powder
3 1/2 oz chocolate chips

UTENSILS
pastry brush
two 13 x 11 inch cookie sheets
waxed paper
scissors
electric beaters
large mixing bowl
sifter
wooden spoon
fork

 Put out everything you need for this recipe on the countertop or table. Turn oven on to moderate 350°F. Brush the cookie sheets with melted butter or oil, line the bases with waxed paper and brush the paper with a little more butter.

1 Using electric beaters, beat butter and sugar in the mixing bowl until mixture is light and creamy.

2 Put in sifted flour and custard powder, stir with the wooden spoon until well mixed.

3 Take one heaped teaspoon of mixture and gently roll into a ball between the palms of your hands. Repeat with the rest of the mixture. Arrange on cookie sheets, allowing room for spreading.

4 Flatten each ball slightly with a fork. Bake for 15 minutes or until the cookies are golden brown. Let them cool on cookie sheets.

5 To decorate the cookies, melt chocolate chips in a bowl over hot water and dip half of each cookie into the chocolate.

Apple Muffins

Preparation time: 20 minutes
Cooking time: 15 minutes **Makes:** about 18

INGREDIENTS
melted butter or oil for
  greasing
1 medium-sized green apple
4 tablespoons butter
3 cups self-rising flour
1 cup sugar
1 egg, lightly beaten
1 cup milk

UTENSILS
pastry brush
three 6-cup muffin pans
potato peeler
sharp knife
sifter
large mixing bowl
wooden spoon
oven mitts

 Put out everything you need on the countertop or table. Turn oven on to moderately hot 415°F. Brush the muffin pans with melted butter or oil.

1 Peel and quarter apple, remove core. Cut apple and butter into 1/4 inch cubes.

2 Sift flour into the mixing bowl. Put in sugar, apple and butter and stir until well mixed. Make a hole in the center.

3 Add combined egg and milk all at once to the dry ingredients. Using a wooden spoon, stir until ingredients are just mixed; do not overbeat.

4 Spoon mixture into muffin pans, filling the cups two-thirds full.

5 Bake 15 minutes or until puffed and browned. Turn onto wire rack to cool. Serve warm with butter.

Make a hole in center of flour mixture and pour in egg and milk all at once.

Breakfast ideas

Pancakes

Preparation time: 5 minutes
Cooking time: 2 minutes per pancake **Makes:** about 10

INGREDIENTS
1 cup all-purpose flour
2 eggs
3/4 cup milk
butter, for greasing

UTENSILS
measuring cups
blender or food processor
small mixing bowl
small frying pan (about
  7 inches)
spatula
plate
dish towel

 Put out everything you need for this recipe on the countertop or table.

1 Place flour, eggs and milk in blender or food processor bowl.

2 Using the pulse action, press button for 10 seconds or until the ingredients are combined and the mixture is not lumpy. Or you can put the flour, eggs and milk into a small bowl and beat with a whisk until all the lumps are gone.

3 Grease the frying pan with butter and pour in 2 tablespoons of mixture. Swirl mixture over base.

4 Cook over medium heat for 1 minute or until the underside is golden. Using a spatula, turn pancake over. Cook other side for 1 minute or until golden. Put cooked pancake on a plate; cover with a dish towel and put out of the way in a warm spot.

5 Cook the rest of the mixture in the same way, greasing the pan when necessary.

Bacon and Eggs

Preparation time: nil
Cooking time: 6 minutes **Serves:** 1

INGREDIENTS
2 teaspoons butter
1 slice bacon,
 with rind cut off
1 egg

UTENSILS
measuring spoon
medium frying pan
cup
spatula
paper towel

 Put out everything you need for this recipe on the countertop or table.

1 Melt butter in frying pan. Add bacon and cook over medium heat for 2 minutes on each side or until lightly browned. Push to the side of the pan.

2 Break the egg into a cup. Reduce heat to low. Slide the egg into pan. Cook for 2 minutes or until it is cooked as you want it. Use a spatula to remove the egg from pan. Drain bacon on a paper towel and place on plate with egg. Serve with toast, if you like.

Notes: People like eggs cooked differently. Some like the yolk runny, others prefer it firm. To test, touch the yolk gently with the back of a spoon to see how firm it is. The longer you cook it, the firmer it becomes. The yolk also goes a pale yellow color when it is firm.

✪ To serve a sausage, cook it in the same way as the bacon, but allow longer. A thin sausage will take about five minutes, a thick one will take about 10 minutes.

✪ To make eggs perfectly round, use a greased egg ring. Place egg ring in pan and slide egg into it.

French Toast

Preparation time: 5 minutes
Cooking time: 2 minutes **Serves:** 2

INGREDIENTS
1 egg
2 tablespoons milk
2 slices raisin bread
2 teaspoons butter

UTENSILS
small bowl
fork
measuring spoons
medium frying pan
spatula

 Put out everything you need for this recipe on the countertop or table.

1 Break egg into a small bowl, add milk and beat lightly with a fork.

2 Dip raisin bread in egg mixture until soaked.

3 Melt butter in frying pan. Place bread in pan. Cook over medium heat for 1 minute or until the underside is golden.

4 Using a spatula, turn bread over. Cook for about 1 minute more. French Toast should be served as soon as it is cooked.

Note: French Toast can be served drizzled with honey or golden syrup or sprinkled with sugar.

Soak slices of raisin bread in egg and milk mixture.

Cook raisin bread on both sides until golden.

Corn Fritters

Preparation time: 15 minutes
Cooking time: 6 minutes **Makes:** 6

INGREDIENTS
$1/2$ cup self-rising flour
10 oz can corn kernels,
  drained
$1/3$ cup grated mature
  Cheddar
2 eggs, lightly beaten
1 tablespoon butter

UTENSILS
measuring cups
measuring spoons
sifter
can opener
large mixing bowl
wooden spoon
medium frying pan
spatula
paper towels

 Put out everything you need for this recipe on the countertop or table.

1 Sift flour into the bowl. Add corn and cheese. Stir until well mixed.

2 Make a hole in the center. Pour eggs into hole, stir until just mixed.

Divide mixture into six equal portions.

3 Melt half the butter in the frying pan. Add three portions of mixture to the pan, about $1 1/4$ inches apart.

4 Cook fritters over medium heat for 3 minutes or until the underside is golden. Turn fritters over with a spatula. Cook other side for about 3 minutes or until golden. Remove from pan; drain on paper towel. Keep warm. Repeat with the rest of the butter and mixture.

Note: Experiment—for example, add one tablespoon of chopped chives or parsley to the mixture, before cooking.

Scrambled Eggs

Preparation time: 5 minutes
Cooking time: 2 minutes **Serves:** 1

INGREDIENTS
2 eggs
2 tablespoons milk
2 teaspoons chopped chives
2 teaspoons butter
2 slices bread
butter for toast

UTENSILS
small mixing bowl
whisk
measuring spoons
small frying pan
  (about 7 inches)
wooden spoon
toaster or broiler
knife

 Put out everything you need for this recipe on the countertop or table.

1 Break eggs into mixing bowl. Add milk and chives; whisk until combined.

2 Melt butter in frying pan. Pour in egg mixture. Stir gently over low heat for 2 minutes or until eggs are set. Don't let them boil.

3 When the eggs are almost cooked, make the toast. Put two slices of bread in the toaster and cook until they are golden on both sides, or place the bread under hot broiler and cook 1—2 minutes on both sides. Spread hot toast with butter; cut into triangles and serve with eggs.

Notes: Be careful not to overcook scrambled eggs as they will become dry and crumbly. Scrambled eggs should be moist, shiny and creamy.

✪ Liven things up by adding two tablespoons grated mature Cheddar or a pinch of dried herbs to the mixture before cooking.

✪ Cook scrambled eggs just before serving.

Ham and Cheese Croissants

Preparation time: 10 minutes
Cooking time: 10 minutes **Serves:** 2

INGREDIENTS
2 croissants
2 slices ham
2 slices mature Cheddar

UTENSILS
sharp knife
baking sheet
oven mitts

 Put out everything you need for this recipe on the countertop or table.
Turn on oven to moderate 350°F.
1 Using a sharp knife, split each croissant open to give two halves. Place croissants cut side up on baking sheet.
2 Cut the ham and cheese slices in half. Top each croissant with a piece of ham and a piece of cheese. Bake for 10 minutes or until the cheese has melted.

Notes: You can get the croissants ready several hours ahead, and cook them just before serving time.
✪ Use either fresh or processed ham slices. Use any cheese, such as swiss or gouda.
✪ Croissants can be bought fresh or frozen from some bakeries.

French Omelet

Preparation time: 2 minutes
Cooking time: 2 minutes **Serves:** 1

INGREDIENTS
2 eggs
2 teaspoons water
2 teaspoons butter

UTENSILS
small mixing bowl
measuring spoon
fork
8 inch frying pan
spatula

 Put out everything you need for this recipe on the countertop or table.

1 Break eggs into the mixing bowl and add water. Beat the eggs with a fork until the whites and yolks are just blended.

2 Melt butter in frying pan until foamy. Tilt pan to spread the butter over its base.

3 Carefully pour eggs into pan and cook over medium heat until mixture has set, tilting pan during cooking to keep the eggs moving.

4 Use a spatula to help fold the omelet. Slide omelet onto the serving plate. Serve immediately.

Tilt the pan gently from time to time to keep the eggs moving while they cook.

Fillings: You can make a filling and add it before folding the omelet. Here are some suggestions:

❂ 1 slice chopped, fried bacon or ham
❂ 6 sliced button mushrooms, fried in 2 teaspoons butter
❂ 2 tablespoons finely grated mature Cheddar.

The Breakfast Tray

Breakfast in bed is a really special treat for Mum or Dad. But be **sure** to ask permission before you boil the water to make tea or coffee.

Tea and Coffee

To make instant coffee or one cup of tea, first put the kettle or jug on to boil. Get out your cup or mug, and put in 1 teaspoon of coffee or 1 tea bag. Take the cup to the kettle, and when the water is boiling, carefully pour it in. Let the tea bag stand for 2 minutes, then take it out with a spoon. Serve milk and sugar separately.

For a pot of tea, measure out 1 teaspoon of tea or 1 tea bag for each cup of boiling water.

After you've poured in water, let tea stand 4–5 minutes, then strain into each cup.

Making Orange Juice

To make one glass of fresh orange juice, you'll need two oranges. You can use any kind of juicer. Make it just before serving time so it won't separate.

Poached Egg on Toast

To poach an egg, fill a small pan with water to about 1¹/4 inches deep. Bring water to boil. Break egg into a cup and slide egg gently into the water.

Turn off the heat, put the lid on the pan, and leave until white is firm and yolk turns white. Lift egg out carefully with a spatula. Serve with buttered toast.

Easy dinners

Chicken and Pasta Salad

Preparation time: 20 minutes
Cooking time: 15 minutes **Serves:** 4

INGREDIENTS
1 cup dried pasta twists
2/3 cup frozen peas
1/2 barbecued chicken
4 oz can corn kernels,
  drained
1 medium red bell pepper,
  chopped
4 green onions, chopped
2 small cucumbers, sliced
1/3 cup bottled Italian
  dressing

UTENSILS
large pan
colander
medium pan
sharp knife
large mixing bowl

 Put out everything you need for this recipe on the countertop or table.

1 Cook pasta twists in a pan of boiling water for about 10 minutes or until they are just tender; drain in colander, rinse under cold water and drain again.

2 Cook peas in medium pan of boiling water for 2 minutes or until tender; drain, rinse under cold water, drain again.

3 Take chicken meat off bones and break meat into small strips.

4 Mix pasta, peas, corn and chicken in the bowl with bell pepper, green onions and cucumber. Add dressing, stir until well mixed.

Note: Serve with a green salad as a main course.
✪ Salad can be made early, covered, and kept in the refrigerator. Add dressing just before serving.

Roast Chicken and Potatoes

Preparation time: 20 minutes
Cooking time: 50 minutes **Serves:** 4

INGREDIENTS

2 lb 7 oz chicken
2 teaspoons butter
1 tablespoon chopped chives
2 teaspoons finely grated
  lemon rind
4 slices bacon, with rind off
6 medium potatoes
2 teaspoons oil
3/4 cup water

UTENSILS

sharp knife
paper towel
measuring spoons and jug
small pan
wooden spoon
pastry brush
vegetable peeler
chopping board
oven mitts
small baking dish
deep baking dish with
  roasting rack

 Put out everything
you need for this
recipe on the
countertop or table. Turn
on oven to moderate

350°F. Cut away any loose
fat from chicken. Wash
chicken thoroughly and
pat dry with paper towel.

1 Melt butter in small pan
over low heat. Take off heat.
Mix in chives and lemon
rind. Brush butter mixture
all over chicken.

2 Lay the bacon slices
in a criss-cross pattern
over the chicken breast.

3 Peel potatoes with a
vegetable peeler. Wash and
pat dry with paper towel.
Cut the potatoes in half
with a sharp knife. Place

**Brush mixture of butter,
chives and lemon rind over
chicken with a pastry brush.**

42

them in the small baking dish and brush well with oil. Place dish in oven.

4 Place chicken on roasting rack in the deep baking dish. Pour water to a depth of $5/8$ inch into the bottom of the dish. Wearing oven mitts, put the chicken in the oven. Bake the chicken and the potatoes for 50 minutes or until the chicken juices are clear when you pierce it with a skewer. The chicken should be golden and the bacon and potatoes crisp. Cut the chicken into pieces to serve. Serve with baked vegetables (pumpkin can be cooked in the same way as the potatoes) and beans.

Salmon Patties

Preparation time: 20 minutes
Cooking time: 6 minutes **Serves:** 4

INGREDIENTS
1 lb potatoes
7 oz can pink salmon, drained
2 tablespoons mayonnaise
4 green onions, chopped
all-purpose flour
1 egg
3/4 cup packaged bread crumbs
1/4 cup oil

UTENSILS
potato peeler
sharp knife
medium pan
colander
large mixing bowl
fork
wooden spoon
small bowl
pastry brush
large frying pan
spatula
paper towel

Put out everything you need for this recipe on the countertop or table.

1 Peel and chop potatoes. Cook in medium pan in boiling water until tender, drain. Put in the mixing bowl and mash with a fork until smooth.

2 Put salmon, mayonnaise and green onions in bowl with potatoes. Stir with wooden spoon until well mixed.

3 Divide mixture into eight portions. Roll each portion into a smooth patty.

4 Dust patties lightly in flour. Beat egg in small bowl, and use to brush patties. Coat in bread crumbs.

5 Heat oil in the frying pan. Put in patties in a single layer; cook over medium heat for 3 minutes or until underside is golden. Use a spatula to turn patties over and cook 3 minutes or until golden. Drain on paper towel. Serve with lemon wedges.

Cheese 'n' Chive Baked Potatoes

Preparation time: 15 minutes
Cooking time: 1¹/4 hours plus 20 minutes **Serves:** 4

INGREDIENTS
4 medium potatoes
¹/4 cup grated mature
  Cheddar
¹/4 cup sour cream
1 tablespoon chopped chives
¹/4 cup grated mature
  Cheddar, extra

UTENSILS
shallow baking dish
oven mitts
sharp knife
spoon
small mixing bowl
fork
grater

 Put out everything you need for this recipe on the countertop or table. Turn the oven on to moderate 350°F.

1 Prick potatoes with a fork and put them in a shallow baking dish. Bake for 1¹/4 hours or until tender. Using oven mitts, remove from oven. Let cool slightly.

2 Using a sharp knife, cut the top one-third off each potato.

3 Using a spoon, scoop potato flesh out of tops and bottoms. Discard the skin of the tops.

4 Put potato flesh in the mixing bowl and mash with a fork until smooth. Add cheese, sour cream and chives. Stir until combined.

5 Spoon potato mixture into potato shells, sprinkle with extra cheese. Put in baking dish. Bake for 20 minutes or until lightly browned.

Spaghetti Bolognese

Preparation time: 5 minutes
Cooking time: 20 minutes **Serves:** 4

INGREDIENTS
2 tablespoons oil
1 large onion, chopped
1 small green bell pepper,
 chopped
2 cloves garlic, crushed
1 lb ground beef
14 oz can tomatoes
2 tablespoons tomato paste
1/2 teaspoon dried oregano
1/2 cup water
13 oz dried spaghetti
grated Parmesan cheese

UTENSILS
2 medium pans
sharp knife
wooden spoon
can opener
fork
colander

 Put out everything you need for this recipe on the countertop or table.

1 Heat oil in a pan. Add onion, bell pepper and garlic and stir-fry over medium heat for 3 minutes or until onion is tender.

2 Add beef; stir-fry over high heat for 3 minutes or until brown.

3 Open can of tomatoes and crush them with a fork. Put in pan with meat and add tomato paste, oregano and water. Bring to boil. Reduce heat to low. Cover and cook for 15 minutes or until sauce has thickened; stir occasionally.

4 While sauce is cooking, bring a pan of water to the boil. Put in spaghetti. Boil for 10 minutes or until tender, drain in a colander.

5 Put spaghetti in serving bowl. Spoon sauce on top and sprinkle with Parmesan cheese.

Note: Add 4 oz sliced mushrooms and fresh herbs, such as chopped basil or parsley, to the sauce for a change.

Satay Lamb

Preparation time: 20 minutes
Cooking time: 10 minutes **Serves:** 4

INGREDIENTS
1¹/₂ lb lamb leg chops
2 tablespoons peanut butter
1 small onion, chopped
¹/₄ cup water
2 teaspoons soy sauce
1 teaspoon curry powder
1 teaspoon grated fresh
  ginger

UTENSILS
wooden skewers
sharp knife
large mixing bowl
food processor or blender
oven mitts

 Put out everything you need for this recipe on the countertop or table. Soak skewers in water until ready to use. Turn broiler on to high.

1 Using a sharp knife, trim bones and fat from the lamb. Cut lamb into ³/₄ inch cubes and put in large mixing bowl.

2 Put peanut butter, onion, water, soy sauce, curry powder and ginger in a blender or food processor bowl and process for 20 seconds or until mixture is smooth. Add to lamb, stir until mixed.

3 Thread lamb onto skewers. Cook under broiler for 10 minutes or until cooked through. Wearing oven mitts, take lamb out to turn and brush occasionally with peanut butter mixture while it is cooking. Serve satays with boiled rice.

Note: Use cubed beef, pork or chicken instead of lamb for this recipe.

Chicken Noodle Stir-fry

Preparation time: 15 minutes plus soaking time
Cooking time: 10 minutes   **Serves:** 4

INGREDIENTS
3 oz packet 2-minute noodles
2 cups boiling water
4 boneless chicken thighs
1 tablespoon cornstarch
2 tablespoons oil
1 tablespoon grated fresh
  ginger
1 clove garlic, crushed
4 cups frozen mixed
  vegetables
1 tablespoon soy sauce
1 teaspoon curry powder

UTENSILS
measuring cup
small mixing bowl
sharp knife
large frying pan
wooden spoon
colander

 Put out everything you need for this recipe on the countertop or table.

1 Put noodles and water in the bowl. Break noodles up and leave for 30 minutes.

2 Cut chicken into thin strips. Toss in cornstarch.

3 Heat oil in the frying pan. Put in chicken strips and stir-fry over high heat for 2 minutes or until lightly browned.

4 Add ginger and garlic, stir-fry for 1 minute. Add vegetables, soy sauce and curry powder, stir-fry for 3 minutes or until tender.

5 Drain noodles. Put them in the pan with vegetables and chicken and stir-fry until heated through.

Note: Use strips of lamb, beef or pork instead of chicken, if you like.

Cook floured chicken strips over high heat for 2 minutes or until browned.

Cakes & desserts

Choc-mint Cone Cakes

Preparation time: 20 minutes
Cooking time: 20 minutes **Makes:** 12

INGREDIENTS
12 oz chocolate cake
 mix
12 flat-bottomed ice-cream
 cones
24 after-dinner mints
12 candy-covered chocolates

UTENSILS
large bowl
wooden spoon
deep 12-cup muffin pan
oven mitts

Read directions on the cake mix packet and put out everything you need on the countertop or table. Turn on oven to moderate 350°F.

1 Prepare cake mix following the directions on the packet.

2 Stand the ice-cream cones in the muffin pan.

3 Put 1 1/2 tablespoons of cake mixture into each cone. Bake for 20 minutes or until the cakes are firm when pressed with the back of a spoon. Wearing oven mitts, take the cakes out of the oven.

4 Put an after-dinner mint on top of each cone cake. Put back in the oven for just 1 minute. Be careful not to overcook the cone cakes after you put the after-dinner mints on top, as they will melt and slide off.

5 Put a candy-covered chocolate on top of each cone cake. Leave the cakes in muffin pan to cool.

Baked Vanilla Custard

Preparation time: 10 minutes
Cooking time: 40 minutes **Serves:** 4

INGREDIENTS
oil, for greasing dish
2 cups milk
3 eggs
1/4 cup sugar
1/4 teaspoon vanilla extract
ground nutmeg, for sprinkling

UTENSILS
2 1/2 cup ovenproof dish
pastry brush
whisk
medium bowl
large baking dish
knife
oven mitts

 Put out everything you need for this recipe on the countertop or table. Turn oven to moderate 350°F. Brush ovenproof dish with oil.

1 Whisk milk, eggs, sugar and vanilla in mixing bowl for 2 minutes.

2 Pour mixture into the greased dish and sprinkle the top with nutmeg.

3 Put the custard dish into a larger baking dish. Pour enough cold water into the baking dish to come halfway up the sides. Bake for 20 minutes, then turn oven down to moderately slow 315°F. Bake 20 minutes more or until custard is set and a knife comes out clean when pushed into the center. Take dish out of water immediately, wearing oven mitts. Serve the baked custard warm or cold, with fruit if you like.

Pour cold water into the baking dish until it comes halfway up the sides.

Custard Orange Cake

Preparation time: 15 minutes
Cooking time: 50 minutes **Makes:** one 9 inch round cake

INGREDIENTS
oil, for greasing pan
2 cups self-rising flour
1/3 cup custard powder
1 1/3 cups sugar
4 tablespoons butter,
  chopped
3 eggs
2 teaspoons finely grated
  orange rind
1 cup orange juice
4 oz cream cheese
2 tablespoons confectioners'
  sugar

UTENSILS
deep 9 inch round cake pan
waxed paper cut to fit bottom
  of cake pan
food processor
wooden spoon
oven mitts
skewer

 Put out everything you need for this recipe on the kitchen bench or table. Turn on oven to moderate 350°F. Brush cake pan with oil. Line base with paper.

1 Sift flour and custard powder and put in food processor bowl with sugar and pieces of butter.

2 Using the pulse action, press the button for 10 seconds or until the mixture is fine and crumbly.

3 Put eggs, orange rind and juice into the food processor bowl. Process for 30 seconds or until smooth.

4 Spoon the mixture into pan; smooth surface. Bake for 50 minutes or until a skewer comes out clean when pushed into middle of cake.

5 Leave cake to stand in the pan for 5 minutes before turning it out onto a wire rack to cool.

6 Mix together cream cheese and confectioners' sugar and spread over top of cake. Decorate with strips of orange rind, if you like.

Strawberry Sundae

Preparation time: 15 minutes
Cooking time: 2 minutes **Serves:** 6

INGREDIENTS
8 oz strawberries
2 tablespoons sugar
1/3 cup orange juice
12 scoops ice-cream
12 ice-cream wafers
1/4 cup chopped walnuts

UTENSILS
food processor
medium saucepan
strainer
ice-cream scoop

 Put out everything you need for this recipe on the countertop or table.

1 Take green tops off strawberries. Put strawberries, sugar and orange juice into food processor bowl. Process for 20 seconds or until mixture is smooth.

2 Pour mixture into saucepan. Bring to boil, boil 1 minute.

3 Put mixture back into processor bowl. Process 10 seconds or until it is smooth; pour through a strainer to strain out seeds; cool.

4 Put ice-cream in serving bowls, pour strawberry sauce over. Decorate with wafers, sprinkle with walnuts. Serve with chocolate cookies and whole strawberries, if you like.

Note: You could use raspberries instead of strawberries, if they're in season.

Scrumptious Chocolate Brownies

Preparation time: 15 minutes
Cooking time: 30 minutes **Makes:** 25

INGREDIENTS
oil, for greasing pan
6¹/₂ oz dark chocolate,
  coarsely chopped
4 tablespoons butter
1 cup light brown sugar,
  firmly packed
¹/₂ cup chopped pecan nuts
2 eggs, lightly beaten
1 cup all-purpose flour

UTENSILS
deep 7¹/₂ inch square
  cake pan
waxed paper
scissors
sharp knife
medium-sized saucepan
sifter
wooden spoon
breadboard
oven mitts

 Put out everything you need for this recipe on the countertop or table. Turn on oven to moderate 350°F. Brush a cake pan with oil.

Cut a strip of waxed paper to fit from top of one side of the pan, across bottom and up opposite side. Grease paper.

1 Put chocolate and butter in saucepan. Stir over low heat with wooden spoon until they have melted. Take off the heat, cool 2 minutes.

2 Add sugar and pecans, stir until well mixed in. Add eggs and mix well. Sift flour, add to the mixture and mix well.

3 Spread the mixture into the greased and papered pan. Bake for 30 minutes or until firm in the center when you press with the back of a spoon.

4 Leave in the pan until cool. Turn out onto a board, cut into squares. Sprinkle with confectioners' sugar.

INDEX